STAR WARS®
WORKBOOKS

1ST GRADE READING

FOR AGES 6–7

BY THE EDITORS OF BRAIN QUEST
CONSULTING EDITOR: TAMIKA JORDAN

WORKMAN PUBLISHING
NEW YORK

Library of Congress Cataloging-in-Publication Data is available.

ISBN: 978-0-7611-7810-1
Workbook series design by Raquel Jaramillo
Cover illustration by Mike Sutfin
Interior illustrations by Lawrence Christmas

Workman books are available at special discounts when purchased in bulk for premiums and sales promotions as well as for fund-raising or educational use. Special editions or book excerpts can also be created to specification. For details, contact the Special Sales Director at the address below, or send an email to specialmarkets@workman.com.

Workman Publishing Co., Inc.
225 Varick Street
New York, NY 10014-4381

workman.com
starwars.com
starwarsworkbooks.com

Printed in the United States of America
First printing June 2014

10 9 8 7 6 5

STAR WARS®
WORKBOOKS

This workbook belongs to:

CEdaR

Anakin on Tatooine

Anakin is at the market. He is looking for supplies to build a droid.

Finish each sentence with one of these **short a** words:

hat

basket

sand

apples

Anakin

planet

Anakin Skywalker is in the market.

He lives on a _Planet_ called Tatooine.

There is a lot of _Sand_ in the desert.

The brown _____ is full of red _____.

It is sunny. Anakin should wear a _____.

Mace Windu's Table

Mace Windu's table is very full.

Finish each sentence with one of these **long a** words:

cage

chain

table

cake

Mace

flame

Mace Windu sits at the blue table.

He has baked a birthday cake for Yoda.

The birthday candle is lit. It has a small flame.

A red bird sits inside a golden cage g.

There is a silver _____ on top of the table.

Boba Fett's Tent

Boba Fett would like to get some rest before his next adventure.

Finish each sentence with one of these **short e** words:

eggs   ten   nest

tent   bed

Boba sits on his _____.

He is inside his _____.

There is a bird's _____ in the tree.

There are _____ in the nest.

How many eggs are there?
There are _____ eggs.

The Queen's Throne Room

Queen Amidala is in her throne room.

Finish each sentence with one of these **long e** words:

Queen   three   feet   beak   reads   green

_____ Amidala sits

on a throne.

Her handmaiden _____

a book.

Her pet bird is

the color _____.

He has yellow _____

and a pink _____.

There are _____ candles

on the small table.

Wicket's Dinner

Wicket is getting ready to eat dinner.

Finish each sentence with one of these **short i** words:

village   sticks   six

fish   dinner

Wicket lives in a _____
on Endor.

It is early evening, time for
_____
_____ .

Wicket uses _____
to make a fire.

How many sticks are there?
_____
_____ .

He cooks a big _____ .

Qui-Gon's Day

Qui-Gon is in the park with his friends.

Finish each sentence with one of these **long i** words:

white   smiles   hide   behind   ice

Qui-Gon _____.

Jar Jar holds a glass filled with _____.

Padmé plays _____-and-seek with Anakin.

Anakin hides _____ a bush.

Padmé wears _____ pants.

Anakin's Mom

Anakin lives with his mother, Shmi, near the city of Mos Espa.

Finish each sentence with one of these **short o** words:

mom sock pot rock hot mop

Anakin's _____
is named Shmi.

Shmi is holding a _____.

There is a big _____ of
soup over the fire.

The fire is very _____.

Anakin is sitting on a
_____.

He is wearing only
one _____.

Yoda's Home

Yoda lives in a hut on the planet Dagobah.

Finish each sentence with one of these **long o** words:

oval   stone   robe   note   toes

Yoda wears a long _____ .

Yoda has six _____ .

Yoda uses the Force to make the _____ float.

The stone is the shape of an _____ .

Yoda is writing a _____ to Mace Windu.

Gungans Have Fun!

These Gungans are having a party.

Finish each sentence with one of these **short u** words:

jumps   umbrella   under

sun   runs

The _____ is shining brightly.

One Gungan _____.

One Gungan _____.

One Gungan sits _____
a red-and-white _____.

Luke's Uniform

Luke Skywalker gets ready to destroy the Death Star.

Finish each sentence with one of these **long u** words:

Luke   blue   human   dune

uniform   cube

_____ Skywalker wears the
_____ of a Rebel pilot.

He stands on top of
a sand _____.

He holds a small _____
in his hand.

It is the color _____.

Luke is a _____ being.

r-blends

When an **r** and another **consonant** are next to each other, you can hear both of their sounds.

Greedo

Here, you can hear both the **g** and the **r** sounds.

You can hear both letters in all the **r-blends** shown here, too:

| cr | br | tr | fr | dr | pr | gr |

Finish each word with one of the **r-blends**.

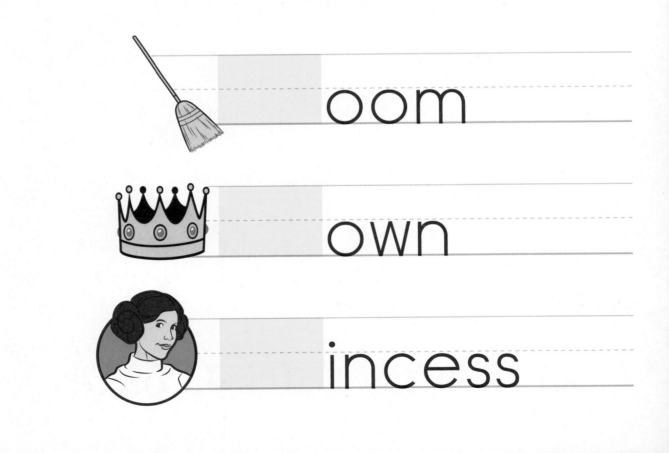

__oom

__own

__incess

____een

____uit

____unk

____oid

____um

____ee

____ievous

l-blends

When an **l** and another **consonant** are next to each other, you can hear both of their sounds.

Plo Koon

Here, you can hear both the **p** and the **l** sounds.

You can hear both letters in all the **l-blends** shown here, too:

pl   gl   sl   cl   bl

Finish each word with one of the **l-blends**.

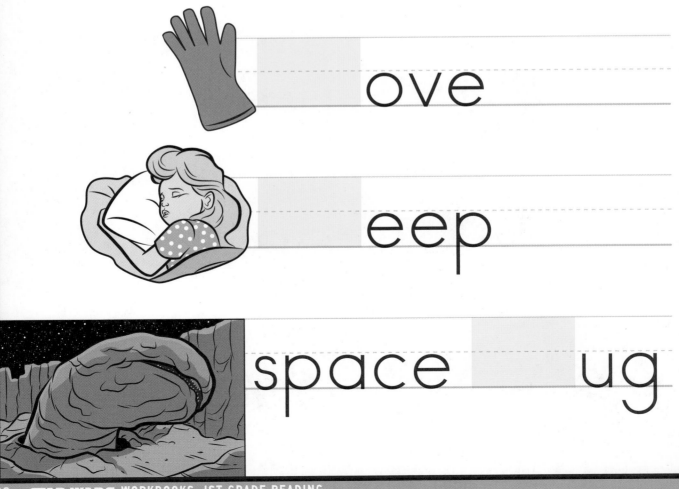

_____ove

_____eep

space_____ug

aws

ate

iers

obe

ack

anket

ones

s-blends

When an **s** and another consonant are next to each other, you can hear both of their sounds.

Skywalker

Here, you can hear both the s and the k sounds.

You can hear both letters in all the s-blends shown here, too:

| sn | sm | sw | sk | sp | st | sc |

Finish each word with one of the **s-blends**.

ile

ull

ider

ar

y

oke

arf

airs

ail

ing

sh and ch

Sometimes two **consonants** that are next to each other combine to make a new sound.

Shmi

Here, the s and the h make the sound sh.

Chewbacca

Here, the c and the h make the sound ch.

Finish each word with one of these letter combinations:

sh   ch

ark

air

eep

erry

eese

ell

eck

irt

ain

aak Ti

th, ph, and wh

Sometimes two **consonants** that are next to each other combine to make a new sound.

 th   The t and the h make the sound th, as in Darth.

 ph   The ph makes the sound f, as in face.

 wh   The wh makes the sound w, as in water.

Finish each word with either **th**, **ph**, or **wh**.

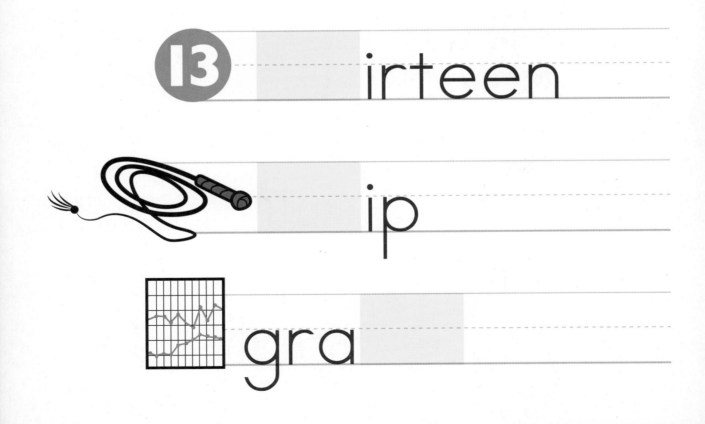

13 ____irteen

____ip

gra____

1,000 ousand

istle

ABCDEFGHI
JKLMNOP
QRSTUVWXYZ
al abet

ale

eel

Dea Star

oto

ay and ai

Sometimes two letters next to each other combine to make one sound.

Aayla

Here, the **a** and the **y** make the **long a** sound.

Ai also makes the **long a** sound.

Finish each sentence with one of these **ay** or **ai** words:

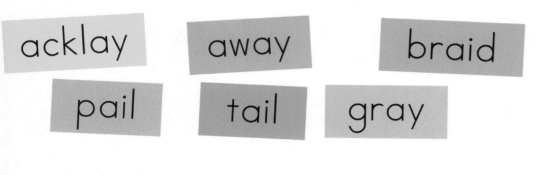

acklay   away   braid

pail   tail   gray

Star Wars takes place a long time ago in a galaxy far, far _____.

The tauntaun has a long _____.

When white gets dirty,
it looks _____ .

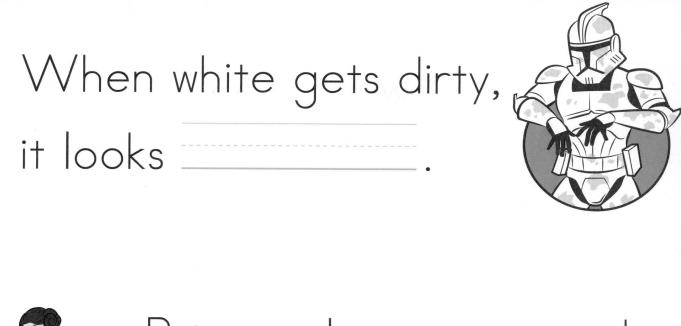

Princess Leia puts sand
in a _____ .

Anakin has one _____ .

This creature is called
an _____ .

ee, ea, and ey

Sometimes two letters next to each other combine to make one sound.

Here, the e and the e make the **long** e sound.

reek

Ea and ey also make the **long** e sound.

Finish each sentence with one of these **ee**, **ea**, or **ey** words:

money

read

dream

teeth

tree

key

Let's _____ a book.

Please brush your _____.

Let's climb up the _____.

You need a _____ to unlock a door.

Queen Amidala has a lot of _____.

When I sleep, I start to _____.

igh and ie

Sometimes two or more letters next to each other combine to make one sound.

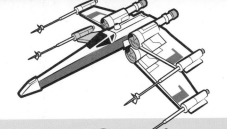

starfighter

Here, the **i**, **g**, and **h** make the **long i** sound.

Ie also makes the **long i** sound.

Finish each sentence with one of these **igh** or **ie** words:

Knight   bright   cries

tie   night   pies

Obi-Wan Kenobi is a Jedi _____.

Please put on your _____.

The sun is _____ .

The youngling _____ .

Look at that stack of delicious _____ .

You can see the moon and stars at _____ .

ow and oa

Sometimes two letters next to each other combine to make one sound.

Owen Lars

Here, the o and the w make the **long o** sound.

Oa also makes the **long o** sound.

Finish each word with one of these letter combinations:

ow   oa

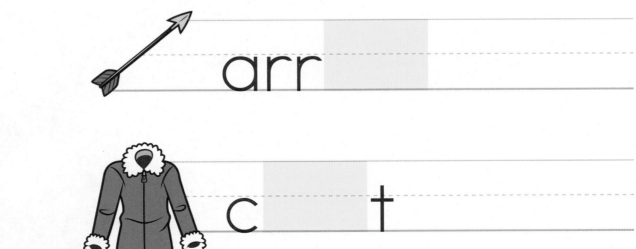

b   t

arr

c   t

r ___

r ___ d

g ___ t

gr ___

fl ___ t

thr ___

bl ___

ui, ue, and ew

Sometimes two letters next to each other combine to make one sound.

juice

Here, the u and the i make the long u sound.

Ue and ew also make the long u sound.

Finish each sentence with one of these **ui**, **ue**, or **ew** words:

fruit   blue   glue

new   flew   suit

Jango _____ away.

His helmet is silver and _____.

The basket is full of _____ .

Luke is wearing a flight _____ .

Anakin has a _____ droid.

C-3PO needs to _____ the broken jar together.

ar and or

When the letters **a** or **o** come before an **r**, their sounds change.

Practice saying and writing the **ar** words below.

Jar Jar

Jar Jar   Jar Jar   Jar Jar

art

far

farm

target

garden

orbit

Practice saying and writing the **or** words below.

orbit _____

corn _____

Sith Lord _____

fort _____

torn _____

Force _____

horn _____

er, ir, and ur

When the letters **e**, **i**, or **u** come before an **r**, their sounds change.

Practice saying and writing the **er**, **ir**, and **ur** words.

Vad**er**

sir _____

fur _____

burn _____

dirt _____

circle _____

Vader _____

girl

fur

herd _____

bird _____

water _____

ruler _____

turn _____

girl _____

surf _____

Soft c and Hard c

The letter **c** makes two different sounds.

The **hard c** makes the **k** sound that you hear in **cat**.

The **soft c** makes the **s** sound that you hear in **city**.

cat

city

Hint: When the letter c is followed by e, i, or y, it is usually a soft c!

Color the cards with a **soft c** word red.

Color the cards with a **hard c** word blue.

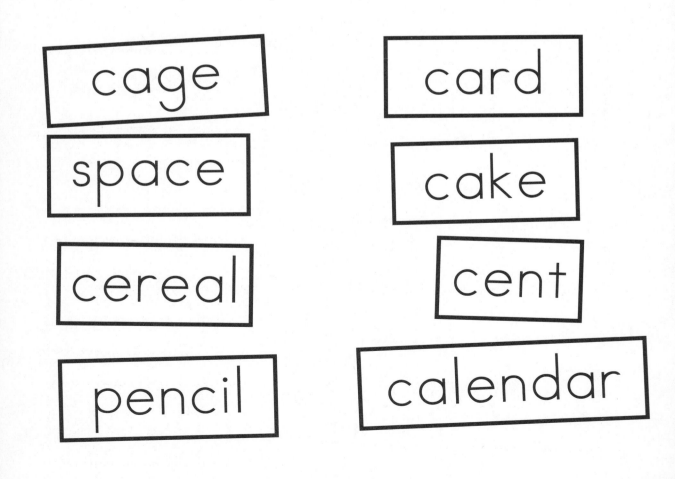

cage

card

space

cake

cereal

cent

pencil

calendar

Soft g and Hard g

The letter **g** makes two different sounds.
The **hard g** makes the first sound that you hear in **goat**.
The **soft g** makes the **j** sound that you hear in **giraffe**.

goat   giraffe

Hint: When the letter g is followed by e, i, or y, it is usually a soft g!

Color the cards with a **soft g** word yellow.
Color the cards with a **hard g** word green.

orange

ago

gentle

energy

game

galaxy

general

good

Naming Words: People

A **noun** is a word for a person, place, or thing.

Finish each sentence with the correct person **noun** from the words below.

boy   son   girl   woman   man

The _____ fixes the droid.

The _____ has blond hair.

The _____ and his _____

are in a landspeeder.

The _____ with red hair

waves hello.

Naming Words: Places

A **noun** is a word for a person, place, or thing.

Finish each sentence with the correct place **noun** from the words below.

forest   mountains   city   lake

desert

The _____ is full
of trees.

The Gungan swims in the
_____
_____.

There are tall buildings in
the _____.

There are sand dunes
in the _____.

There is snow on top of
the _____.

Naming Words: Things

A **noun** is a word for a person, place, or thing.

Finish each sentence with the correct thing **noun** from the words below.

hammer   nails   droid   goggles

Anakin builds a _____ .

He wears _____ to
protect his eyes.

He holds a _____ .

He has a box of _____ .

Proper Naming Words

A **proper noun** is the name of a specific person, place, or thing.

Proper nouns always begin with a capital letter.

Underline the **proper nouns** in each sentence.

Han flies the *Millennium Falcon.*

Chewbacca is tall and hairy.

The Death Star is big.

Luke lives on Tatooine.

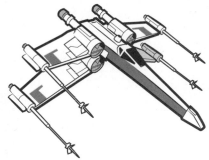 The X-wing is fast.

Wicket lives on Endor.

Go, Wookiee, Go!

A **verb** is an action word. It tells what someone or something does.

Circle the **verb** in each sentence.

The Wookiee eats.

The Wookiee sleeps.

The Wookiee waves.

The Wookiee climbs.

The Wookiee runs.

The Wookiee builds a droid.

Describe the Creatures!

Read the **adjectives** in the word boxes.

Write the best **adjective** to tell about each picture.

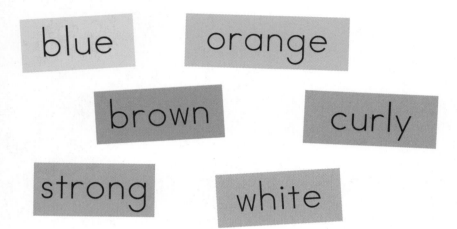

blue   orange

brown   curly

strong   white

The Twi'lek has _____ skin and horns.

The _____ Gungan lives on Naboo.

The bantha has

_____

_____ horns.

The

_____

_____

wampa lives on Hoth.

The

_____

_____

Wookiee is fierce.

The _____ tauntaun

carries heavy loads.

The Youngling's Adventure!

A **sentence** is a group of words that tells a complete thought. All sentences begin with a **capital letter**. A **statement** is a sentence that tells what someone or something does. A **statement** ends with a period.

Read this **sentence**:

The orange youngling runs.

Circle the **noun**. Underline the **verb**.

Draw a rectangle around the **adjective**.

Draw a triangle around the **capital letter** that begins the sentence.

Draw a square around the **period** that ends the sentence.

Now copy the sentence below.

Circle the **noun** in this sentence:

The youngling walks.

Underline the **verb** in this sentence:

The youngling sits.

Draw a rectangle around the **adjective** in this sentence:

The youngling is sleepy.

Draw a triangle around the **capital letter** that begins this sentence. Draw a square around the **period** that ends this sentence:

A friend sees the youngling.

The Youngling's Day!

These sentences are written incorrectly.

Write each sentence correctly.

the youngling sings.

dances the youngling

the runs youngling

The youngling jumps

the youngling sleeps

youngling dives. The

Yoda Questions

Some sentences ask a **question.** A **question** begins with a **capital letter** and ends with a **question mark.** Some questions start with **question words**, such as:

who   what   when   where   why   how

Read each question. Circle the **question word**.

What is Yoda wearing?

Who is Yoda talking to?

Where is Yoda?

How does Yoda look?

When will Yoda go to sleep?

Why is Yoda green?

These sentences are written incorrectly.

Write each sentence correctly.

when will Yoda sit down

_____

_____

what color is Yoda?

_____

_____

how old is Yoda

_____

_____

who is talking to Yoda

_____

_____

This is Yoda

Read about Yoda.

Then answer the questions on the next page.

This is Yoda. Yoda is a Jedi Master.

Yoda is green. He is very old.

Yoda lives in a hut. He uses the Force.

What is Yoda?

Yoda is a _____.

What color is Yoda?

Yoda is _____.

Where does Yoda live?

Yoda lives in a _____.

What does Yoda use?

Yoda uses the _____.

Jawas

Read about Jawas.

Then answer the questions on the next page.

Jawas live in the desert.

They wear brown robes with hoods.

They buy and sell old droids.

These Jawas are fixing some old droids.

The small droid is red and the big droid is blue.

Where do Jawas live?

Jawas live in the _____.

What do Jawas buy and sell?

Jawas buy and sell _____.

What color is the big droid?

The big droid is _____.

What color is the small droid?

The small droid is _____.

Luke Skywalker

Read about Luke.

Then answer the questions on the next page.

Luke Skywalker lives on a desert planet called Tatooine.

He lives on a farm with his aunt and uncle.

He knows that his father was a Jedi Knight.

He does not know that his father's name is Darth Vader.

What is Luke's last name?

Luke's last name is

_____

_ _ _ _ _ _ _ _ _ _ _ _ _ _

_____ .

Where does Luke live?

Luke lives on the planet

_____

_ _ _ _ _ _ _ _ _ _ _ _ _ _

_____ .

Who is Luke's father?

Luke's father is

_____ _____

_ _ _ _ _ _ _ _ _ _ _ _ _ _

_____ _____ .

Princess Leia

Read about Leia.

Then finish the questions on the next page.

Princess Leia sends a message to Obi-Wan Kenobi.

"Help me, Obi-Wan Kenobi!" she says. "You're my only hope."

She puts the message inside R2-D2.

She tells R2-D2 to find Obi-Wan Kenobi and deliver the message.

R2-D2 escapes. He travels to Tatooine to look for Obi-Wan Kenobi.

Put an X in the box with the correct answer.

Who does Princess Leia send a message to?

☐ Obi-Wan Kenobi   ☐ R2-D2   ☐ Darth Vader

Where does R2-D2 travel to find Obi-Wan Kenobi?

☐ Tatooine   ☐ R2-D2   ☐ Message

What is the name of her droid?

☐ Obi-Wan Kenobi   ☐ R2-D2   ☐ Tatooine

R2-D2 and C-3PO

Read about R2-D2 and C-3PO.

Then finish the sentences on the next page.

R2-D2 and C-3PO are droids. R2-D2 is small. The top part of his body is silver and blue. The bottom is white and blue. C-3PO is a tall droid. He is the color gold. He can speak more than six million different languages. R2-D2 and C-3PO have many adventures together. They are friends.

R2-D2 is a type of _____.

C-3PO is not a small droid.
He is _____.

R2-D2 is _____
and blue and white.

C-3PO is the color _____.

R2-D2 and C-3PO are very
good _____.

Han Solo

Read about Han Solo.

Then write **true** or **false** for the statements on the next page.

Han Solo is a pilot. His starship is called the *Millennium Falcon*. It is very fast. It zooms through the galaxy.

Han Solo flies the *Millennium Falcon* through an asteroid belt. He has to be careful! He can't let an asteroid hit his starship!

Han Solo is a pilot.

The name of Han Solo's starship is the *Millennium Falcon.*

Han Solo does not want an asteroid to hit his starship.

The *Millennium Falcon* is a slow starship.

Chewbacca's World

Read about Chewbacca's world.

Then finish the sentences on the next page.

Chewbacca is a Wookiee. He is very tall and has brown fur. His best friend is Han Solo.

Wookiees come from a jungle planet. It is called Kashyyyk. All Wookiees are very strong.

Wookiees are loyal and gentle friends. When Wookiees get mad, they can be very fierce. You should never make a Wookiee mad at you!

Chewbacca is a very tall

_____

_____ .

Chewbacca has _____ fur.

Chewbacca's best friend
is _____ .

Wookiees are good friends
because they are loyal and

_____

_____ .

When Wookiees are mad,
they can be _____ .

The Jedi Knights

Read about the Jedi Knights.

Then answer the questions on the next page.

Jedi Knights use the Force to protect the galaxy. They have many talents. They are strong and wise. They are very brave.

Jedi Knights live by the Jedi Code, which says that they can only use the Force for good things. They come from all over the galaxy. Obi-Wan Kenobi, Aayla Secura, and Mace Windu are all Jedi Knights.

What do Jedi Knights use to protect the galaxy?

They use the _____.

What do Jedi Knights live by?

They live by the _____

_____.

What are the names of the three Jedi Knights in the picture?

The Jedi Knights are:

_____

_____

_____.

Darth Vader and the Force

Read about Darth Vader.

Then finish the statements on the next page.

Darth Vader was once a Jedi Knight, but he turned to the dark side of the Force. He is very strong. He can use the Force to destroy things. This is not a good use of the Force.

Darth Vader uses a red lightsaber. He wears a black robe and a black helmet. He is very tall. When he walks through his starship, the stormtroopers are all afraid of him. Why are they afraid? They are afraid because Darth Vader can destroy them.

Darth Vader is on the
_____ _____ side of the Force.

The color of Darth Vader's
lightsaber is _____ .

Darth Vader's helmet is
_____ .

The soldiers fear Darth
Vader because he can
_____
_____ .

Lightsabers

Read about lightsabers.

Then answer the questions on the next page.

Lightsabers are blades of pure energy. They can cut through anything—except other lightsabers.

Jedi Knights make their own lightsabers. They use special crystals to give them energy. The color of the crystal is what gives the lightsaber its color.

Yoda carries a green lightsaber. Obi-Wan Kenobi's lightsaber is blue. Darth Vader has a red lightsaber.

What is a lightsaber made of?

What gives a lightsaber its color?

What color is Yoda's lightsaber?

Who carries a red lightsaber?

Who has a blue lightsaber?

Boba Fett

Read about Boba Fett.

Then finish the sentences on the next page.

Boba Fett is a bounty hunter. He wears green armor and carries a blaster. His armor is very special. It lets him do many things that other people cannot do. He can fly with his jetpack. He can also shoot flames.

Boba Fett is very smart. He doesn't talk a lot, though. His father was Jango Fett. Jango was also a bounty hunter.

Boba loved his father and wanted to grow up to be just like him. Now Boba works for Jabba the Hutt. Jabba wants Boba to find Han Solo. If Boba captures Han, Jabba will give him a reward.

Boba Fett is a

_____

_____ hunter.

The color of Boba's

armor is _____

_____.

Boba Fett can _____

_____

with his jetpack.

Jango Fett was Boba's

_____

_____.

Boba is looking for

_____

_____.

Lando and Lobot

Read the sentences.

Write the correct **feeling word** to finish each sentence.

Lando eats a delicious apple.

Lando is _____.

hungry   angry

Lobot lost one of his boots.

Lobot is _____.

upset   excited

Lando sees Darth Vader.

Lando is _____.

scared   glad

Lobot has worked all day and wants to go to bed.

Lobot is _____.

sleepy   shy

Lando can't wait to see his friend Han Solo.

Lando is _____.

sad   excited

Lando helps Han Solo escape from Darth Vader.

Lando is _____.

tired   proud

Answers

__Anakin__ Skywalker is in the market.

He lives on a __planet__ called Tatooine.

There is a lot of __sand__ in the desert.

The brown __basket__ is full of red __apples__.

It is sunny. Anakin should wear a __hat__.

__Mace__ Windu sits at the blue __table__.

He has baked a birthday __cake__ for Yoda.

The birthday candle is lit. It has a small __flame__.

A red bird sits inside a golden __cage__.

There is a silver __chain__ on top of the table.

Boba sits on his __bed__.

He is inside his __tent__.

There is a bird's __nest__ in the tree.

There are __eggs__ in the nest.

How many eggs are there? There are __ten__ eggs.

__Queen__ Amidala sits on a throne.

Her handmaiden __reads__ a book.

Her pet bird is the color __green__.

He has yellow __feet__ and a pink __beak__.

There are __three__ candles on the small table.

Wicket lives in a __village__ on Endor.

It is early evening, time for __dinner__.

Wicket uses __sticks__ to make a fire.

How many sticks are there? __six__.

He cooks a big __fish__.

Qui-Gon __smiles__.

Jar Jar holds a glass filled with __ice__.

Padmé plays __hide__ - and-seek with Anakin.

Anakin hides __behind__ a bush.

Padmé wears __white__ pants.

Anakin's __mom__ is named Shmi.

Shmi is holding a __mop__.

There is a big __pot__ of soup over the fire.

The fire is very __hot__.

Anakin is sitting on a __rock__.

He is wearing only one __sock__.

Yoda wears a long __robe__.

Yoda has six __toes__.

Yoda uses the Force to make the __stone__ float.

The stone is the shape of an __oval__.

Yoda is writing a __note__ to Mace Windu.

The __sun__ is shining brightly.

One Gungan __runs__.

One Gungan __jumps__.

One Gungan sits __under__ a red-and-white __umbrella__.

__Luke__ Skywalker wears the __uniform__ of a Rebel pilot.

He stands on top of a sand __dune__.

He holds a small __cube__ in his hand.

It is the color __blue__.

Luke is a __human__ being.

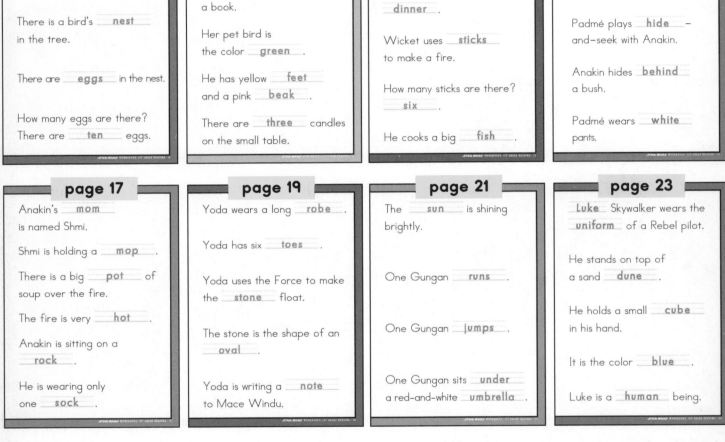

r-blends

When an r and another **consonant** are next to each other, you can hear both of their sounds.

Greedo

Here, you can hear both the g and the r sounds.

You can hear both letters in all the **r-blends** shown here, too:

cr br tr fr dr pr gr

Finish each word with one of the **r-blends**.

b**r**oom
c**r**own
p**r**incess

green
fruit
trunk
d**r**oid
d**r**um
tree
grievous

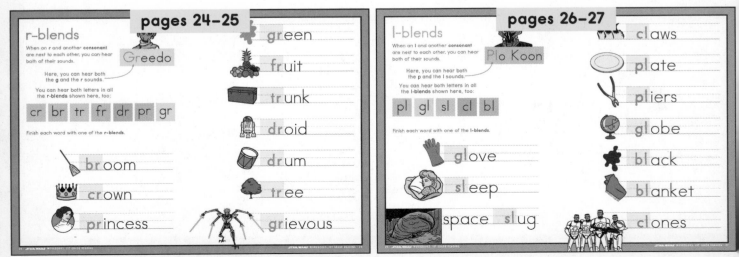

l-blends

When an l and another **consonant** are next to each other, you can hear both of their sounds.

Plo Koon

Here, you can hear both the p and the l sounds.

You can hear both letters in all the **l-blends** shown here, too:

pl gl sl cl bl

Finish each word with one of the **l-blends**.

glove
sleep
space **sl**ug

c**l**aws
plate
pliers
globe
b**l**ack
b**l**anket
c**l**ones

pages 28–29

s–blends

When an s and another consonant are next to each other, you can hear both of their sounds.

Skywalker

Here, you can hear both the s and the k sounds.

You can hear both letters in all the s-blends shown here, too:

sn sm sw sk sp st sc

Finish each word with one of the s-blends.

smile
skull
spider
star
sky
smoke
scarf
stairs
snail
swing

pages 30–31

sh and ch

Sometimes two consonants that are next to each other combine to make a new sound.

Shmi — Here, the s and the h make the sound sh.

Chewbacca — Here, the c and the h make the sound ch.

Finish each word with one of these letter combinations: sh ch

shark
chair
sheep
cherry
cheese
shell
check
shirt
chain
Shaak Ti

pages 32–33

th, ph, and wh

Sometimes two consonants that are next to each other combine to make a new sound.

Darth

th The t and the h make the sound th, as in Darth.

ph The ph makes the sound f, as in face.

wh The wh makes the sound w, as in water.

Finish each word with either th, ph, or wh.

thirteen
whip
graph
thousand
whistle
alphabet
whale
wheel
Death Star
photo

pages 34–35

ay and ai

Sometimes two letters next to each other combine to make one sound.

Aayla

Here, the a and the y make the long a sound.

Ai also makes the long a sound.

Finish each sentence with one of these ay or ai words:

acklay away braid pail tail gray

Star Wars takes place a long time ago in a galaxy far, far away.

The tauntaun has a long tail.

When white gets dirty, it looks gray.

Princess Leia puts sand in a pail.

Anakin has one braid.

This creature is called an acklay.

pages 36–37

ee, ea, and ey

Sometimes two letters next to each other combine to make one sound.

reek

Here, the e and the e make the long e sound.

Ea and ey also make the long e sound.

Finish each sentence with one of these ee, ea, or ey words:

money read dream teeth tree key

Let's read a book.

Please brush your teeth.

Let's climb up the tree.

You need a key to unlock a door.

Queen Amidala has a lot of money.

When I sleep, I start to dream.

pages 38–39

igh and ie

Sometimes two or more letters next to each other combine to make one sound.

starfighter

Here, the i, g, and h make the long i sound.

Ie also makes the long i sound.

Finish each sentence with one of these igh or ie words:

Knight bright cries tie night pies

Obi-Wan Kenobi is a Jedi Knight.

Please put on your tie.

The sun is bright.

The youngling cries.

Look at that stack of delicious pies.

You can see the moon and stars at night.

pages 40–41

ow and oa

Sometimes two letters next to each other combine to make one sound.

Owen Lars

Here, the o and the w make the long o sound.

Oa also makes the long o sound.

Finish each word with one of these letter combinations: ow oa

boat
arrow
coat
row
road
goat
grow
float
throw
blow

pages 42–43

ui, ue, and ew

Sometimes two letters next to each other combine to make one sound.

juice

Here, the u and the i make the long u sound.

Ue and ew also make the long u sound.

Finish each sentence with one of these ui, ue, or ew words:

fruit blue glue new flew suit

Jango flew away.

His helmet is silver and blue.

The basket is full of fruit.

Luke is wearing a flight suit.

Anakin has a new droid.

C-3PO needs to glue the broken jar together.

Answers

ar and or

When the letters a or o come before an r, their sounds change.
Practice saying and writing the **ar** words below.

Jar Jar

Jar Jar **Jar Jar   Jar Jar**

art **art**

far **far**

farm **farm**

target **target**

garden **garden**

Practice saying and writing the **or** words below.

orbit

orbit **orbit**

corn **corn**

Sith Lord **Sith Lord**

fort **fort**

torn **torn**

Force **Force**

horn **horn**

---

er, ir, and ur

When the letters e, i, or u come before an r, their sounds change.
Practice saying and writing the **er, ir,** and **ur** words.

Vader   girl   fur

sir **sir**

fur **fur**

burn **burn**

dirt **dirt**

circle **circle**

Vader **Vader**

herd **herd**

bird **bird**

water **water**

ruler **ruler**

turn **turn**

girl **girl**

surf **surf**

Soft c and Hard c

The letter c makes two different sounds.
The **hard c** makes the **k** sound that you hear in **cat**.
The **soft c** makes the **s** sound that you hear in **city**.

cat   city

Hint: When the letter c is followed by e, i, or y, it is usually a soft c!

Color the cards with a **soft c** word red.
Color the cards with a **hard c** word blue.

cage   card
space   cake
cereal   cent
pencil   calendar

Soft g and Hard g

The letter g makes two different sounds.
The **hard g** makes the first sound that you hear in **goat**.
The **soft g** makes the **j** sound that you hear in **giraffe**.

goat   giraffe

Hint: When the letter g is followed by e, i, or y, it is usually a soft g!

Color the cards with a **soft g** word yellow.
Color the cards with a **hard g** word green.

orange   ago
gentle   energy
game   galaxy
general   good

Naming Words: People

A **noun** is a word for a person, place, or thing.
Finish each sentence with the correct person **noun** from the words below.

boy   son   girl   woman   man

The **girl** fixes the droid.

The **woman** has blond hair.

The **man** and his **son** are in a landspeeder.

The **boy** with red hair waves hello.

The **forest** is full of trees.

The Gungan swims in the **lake**.

There are tall buildings in the **city**.

There are sand dunes in the **desert**.

There is snow on top of the **mountains**.

Anakin builds a **droid**.

He wears **goggles** to protect his eyes.

He holds a **hammer**.

He has a box of **nails**.

Proper Naming Words

A **proper noun** is the name of a specific person, place, or thing.
Proper nouns always begin with a capital letter.
Underline the **proper nouns** in each sentence.

Han flies the _Millennium Falcon_.

Chewbacca is tall and hairy.

The Death Star is big.

Luke lives on Tatooine.

The X-wing is fast.

Wicket lives on Endor.

Go, Wookiee, Go!

A **verb** is an action word. It tells what someone or something does.
Circle the **verb** in each sentence.

The Wookiee (eats).

The Wookiee (sleeps).

The Wookiee (waves).

The Wookiee (climbs).

The Wookiee (runs).

The Wookiee (builds) a droid.

Describe the Creatures!

Read the **adjectives** in the word boxes.
Write the best **adjective** to tell about each picture.

blue orange
brown curly
strong white

The bantha has __curly__ horns.

The __white__ wampa lives on Hoth.

The Twi'lek has __blue__ skin and horns.

The __brown__ Wookiee is fierce.

The __orange__ Gungan lives on Naboo.

The __strong__ tauntaun carries heavy loads.

The Youngling's Adventure!

A **sentence** is a group of words that tells a complete thought. All sentences begin with a **capital letter**. A **statement** is a sentence that tells what someone or something does. A **statement** ends with a period.

Read this **sentence**:

The orange youngling runs.

Circle the **noun**. Underline the **verb**.
Draw a rectangle around the **adjective**.
Draw a triangle around the **capital letter** that begins the sentence.
Draw a square around the **period** that ends the sentence.
Now copy the sentence below.

The youngling walks.

Underline the **verb** in this sentence:

The youngling sits.

Draw a rectangle around the **adjective** in this sentence:

The youngling is sleepy.

Draw a triangle around the **capital letter** that begins this sentence. Draw a square around the **period** that ends this sentence:

A friend sees the youngling.

The Youngling's Day!

These sentences are written incorrectly.
Write each sentence correctly.

the youngling sings.
__The youngling sings.__

dances the youngling
__The youngling dances.__

the runs youngling
__The youngling runs.__

The youngling jumps
__The youngling jumps.__

the youngling sleeps
__The youngling sleeps.__

youngling dives. The
__The youngling dives.__

Yoda Questions

Some sentences ask a **question**. A question begins with a **capital letter** and ends with a **question mark**. Some questions start with **question words**, such as:

who what when where why how

Read each question. Circle the **question word**.

(What) is Yoda wearing?
(Who) is Yoda talking to?
(Where) is Yoda?
(How) does Yoda look?
(When) will Yoda go to sleep?
(Why) is Yoda green?

These sentences are written incorrectly.
Write each sentence correctly.

when will Yoda sit down
__When will Yoda sit down?__

what color is Yoda?
__What color is Yoda?__

how old is Yoda
__How old is Yoda?__

who is talking to Yoda
__Who is talking to Yoda?__

What is Yoda?
Yoda is a __Jedi Master__.

What color is Yoda?
Yoda is __green__.

Where does Yoda live?
Yoda lives in a __hut__.

What does Yoda use?
Yoda uses the __Force__.

Where do Jawas live?
Jawas live in the __desert__.

What do Jawas buy and sell?
Jawas buy and sell __droids__.

What color is the big droid?
The big droid is __blue__.

What color is the small droid?
The small droid is __red__.

What is Luke's last name?
Luke's last name is __Skywalker__.

Where does Luke live?
Luke lives on the planet __Tatooine__.

Who is Luke's father?
Luke's father is __Darth Vader__.

Put an X in the box with the correct answer.

Who does Princess Leia send a message to?
☒ Obi-Wan Kenobi ☐ R2-D2 ☐ Darth Vader

Where does R2-D2 travel to find Obi-Wan Kenobi?
☒ Tatooine ☐ R2-D2 ☐ Message

What is the name of her droid?
☐ Obi-Wan Kenobi ☒ R2-D2 ☐ Tatooine

R2-D2 is a type of __droid__.

C-3PO is not a small droid.
He is __tall__.

R2-D2 is __silver__ and blue and white.

C-3PO is the color __gold__.

R2-D2 and C-3PO are very good __friends__.

Han Solo is a pilot. __true__

The name of Han Solo's starship is the *Millennium Falcon*. __true__

Han Solo does not want an asteroid to hit his starship. __true__

The *Millennium Falcon* is a slow starship. __false__

Chewbacca is a very tall __Wookiee__.

Chewbacca has __brown__ fur.

Chewbacca's best friend is __Han Solo__.

Wookiees are good friends because they are loyal and __gentle__.

When Wookiees are mad, they can be __fierce__.

What do Jedi Knights use to protect the galaxy?
They use the __Force__.

What do Jedi Knights live by?
They live by the __Jedi Code__.

What are the names of the three Jedi Knights in the picture?
The Jedi Knights are:
__Obi-Wan Kenobi, Aayla Secura, and Mace Windu__

Answers

page 85

Darth Vader is on the ___dark___ side of the Force.

The color of Darth Vader's lightsaber is ___red___.

Darth Vader's helmet is ___black___.

The soldiers fear Darth Vader because he can ___destroy them___

page 87

What is a lightsaber made of? ___pure energy___

What gives a lightsaber its color? ___special crystals___

What color is Yoda's lightsaber? ___green___

Who carries a red lightsaber? ___Darth Vader___

Who has a blue lightsaber? ___Obi-Wan Kenobi___

page 89

Boba Fett is a ___bounty___ hunter.

The color of Boba's armor is ___green___.

Boba Fett can ___fly___ with his jetpack.

Jango Fett was Boba's ___father___.

Boba is looking for ___Han Solo___.

pages 90–91

Lando and Lobot

Read the sentences.
Write the correct **feeling word** to finish each sentence.

Lando eats a delicious apple.
Lando is ___hungry___.
hungry   angry

Lobot lost one of his boots.
Lobot is ___upset___.
upset   excited

Lando sees Darth Vader.
Lando is ___scared___.
scared   glad

Lobot has worked all day and wants to go to bed.
Lobot is ___sleepy___.
sleepy   shy

Lando can't wait to see his friend Han Solo.
Lando is ___excited___.
sad   excited

Lando helps Han Solo escape from Darth Vader.
Lando is ___proud___.
tired   proud